Couples

Michael Stewart was born in Salford in 1971. His debut novel *King Crow* won The Guardian's 'Not the Booker' Prize, and was the only debut selected as a 'recommended read' for World Book Night 2012. His poetry has featured in a range of magazines and anthologies.

He was writer in residence at Theatre in the Mill, Bradford, from 2005-2008, and is now senior lecturer in Creative Writing at the University of Huddersfield. He is also the editor of the celebrated series of Grist anthologies. He lives with his partner and son in Bradford.

Couples

MICHAEL STEWART

VALLEY

First published 2013 by Valley Press
Woodend, The Crescent, Scarborough, YO11 2PW
www.valleypressuk.com

ISBN: 978 1 908853 22 6
Cat. no. VP0042

Cover photograph by David Ruston / Rusty Imaging
with thanks to Charlotte Middleton

9 8 7 6 5 4 3 2 1

A CIP record for this book is
available from the British Library

Printed and bound in Great Britain by
Imprint Digital, Upton Pyne, Exeter

www.valleypressuk.com/authors/michaelstewart

for Joan and Ted

(Left) Contents

Contents (Right)

Acknowl

'Your Bath' was previously published as 'Bath'
in *HQ Poetry*; 'Couples' in *Albatross*; 'Clean' in
Not Only The Dark (Categorical Books, 2011)
and 'The Meaning Of Life' in *Orbis*.

edgements

Many thanks to David Gill, Jim Greenhalf
and Gaia Holmes. Big thanks also to
A.L. Kennedy and Jamie McGarry.

He

He started buying Valium off the internet
at four pound a pop,
fifty at a time, until
he had five hundred pills
which he kept in a locked cupboard.

One day when his wife was at work
and his kids at school
he took a brush
and a pot of paint
and decorated the kitchen
so that everything was blue.
The floor, the units, the fridge,
the plates, the knives, the kettle.

He left a note
to his wife and two daughters.
The note was also blue.
It said: I love you.

She

She came home to the mess he'd made,
the paint still wet,
the kitchen stinking of paint.

She closed the door behind her,
her hands now stained with thick blue gloss.
She didn't see the note,
walked through the house
shouting his name.
She ran into their bedroom,
it was too late for 999.

That was two years ago.

Now she's moved on.
Met a man through Matchmaker dot com.
But sometimes when everyone is out,
she sits at the kitchen table,
blue all around her,
and blue inside.

Clean

She scrubs the taps with Ajax,
she bleaches the bath with Domestos,
she scours the bowl with vinegar and wire.
On her hands and knees, she rubs
the stains from the wood.

She takes the sheets
and the covers from the seats
and soaks them in a pint of Parazone.
She polishes the glass with a linen scrim
and spray gun of Windolene.

Then she takes a brush to her nails
and rubs until they bleed.
Her work is done, it's over
now everything inside is clean,
no one would know he'd even been.

The Spring Fires

They found him burning furniture in the back yard.
First the dining table, faux-antique oak
and the chairs, with legs like varicose veins.
He piled up the kitchen units,
the work bench and the foot stool.
Next to go, the sofa and the armchair,
a matching set from DFS.
The glazed dresser and the sideboard, both solid teak,
a pine chest, a shelving unit from Ikea, a wicker fruit bowl,
a stirring spoon and an ash wine rack,
the white wood tallboy with its drawers of MDF,
a walnut bureau, a wedding gift,
his grandma's rocking chair, an heirloom.

Last to go, the double bed,
their bed, its base first then its headrest,
then the mattress and the duvet.
What a gagging stink that made,
the bed they'd shared all these years
a thick fog of black smoke.

It's over, they said, *there's nothing left.*
I know, he said, and lit a cigarette.

Offal

Monday's tea was cold white tripe and vinegar.
Tuesday: onions and liver.
Wednesday: black pudding and mushy peas.
Thursday: Greasy Reany's scraps:
caul fat and battered faggots.
Friday was a feast
of pig's trotters, fried kidneys
cow heel, ox tongue and sheep entrails.

On Saturday he had a green salad.
On Sunday bile and brown ale.
It was a balanced diet
and he lived until he was ninety five.
When asked for his secret
he said: never marry,
never retire,
drink whisky every day,
and eat tripe –
don't swallow it.

Swine

She started gaining weight when she got pregnant,
pound by pound, week by week,
gorging on Jersey cream and treacle pudding.
Deep fried pizza was her favourite
washed down with a tin of Iron Bru,
Dime bars, cheesy Doritos and Häagen-Dazs.
Fried bacon and fried bread,
Big Macs and Butterkist popcorn.
Taramasalata with brandy butter,
Scotch eggs and Bockwurst.
In the pub it was Pepperami and pork scratchings,
dry roasted nuts and Melton Mowbray pies.

She gave birth to a healthy boy, seven pounds and four ounces.
The scales hardly registered the difference.
In nine months she'd put on six stone,
ten months later another seven.
When she couldn't get up the stairs
she got a commode.
When she couldn't get out of her chair
she got home help.
Now she sits all day
drinking R White's lemonade
and scoffing Milk Tray.
She watches *Judge Judy* and *Cash in the Attic*,
Loose Women and *Lonely Planet*.
As for her son, he's doing fine
on the farm, among swine.

Couples

Some are tent poles
propping each other up,
one falls over and the other topples,
that's no good.

Other couples are stuck;
two pawns meeting
down the same file.
They'll never budge till a piece
comes and knocks them off.

Then there are the couples
who live in the same house,
eat at the same table,
sleep in the same bed
but they're two opposing magnets.

They can't see it but they can feel
the push every time they touch.

There are other couples
walking around parks, travelling on buses,
clinging, frightened, quietly frantic,
or standing next to each other,
two sheep in a field
chewing, chewing, chewing
until at last they can swallow.

You And Me

You eat an apple an orange and a banana every morning.
I drink a bottle of red and four pints of stout every evening.
You only drink water from Sainte-Catherine spring.
I only drink water if I've just been sick.

You eat wheat germ and linseed and organic cranberries.
I eat lime pickle and fried egg sandwiches.
You say your angel is enshrined in light,
your angel guides you to your Pilates.

My angel only comes out at night.
He whispers that I'm ill, mad and dying.
You wrote 'I love you' with sugar on the kitchen tiles.
I spilt salt in the goldfish bowl and then lied.

You never drink and drive.
I always have the requisite two pints.
You go your way and I'll go mine
and we will meet at the end of time.

Him

he only felt loved
after sex sex for him
was his lover giving
herself to him and
proving her feelings
and his gift to her to
connect with her
inside and make her
alive with pleasure
two people becoming
one person albeit for
only a breath this was
how he felt loved

they went to therapy sessions and read self-help manuals
talking until dawn

Her

she would only have
sex if she felt loved
when he came to her
strong with feeling
stroking her hair and
kissing her neck he
was using her she
would push him away
she had to feel loved
she'd say before she
would get undressed
and lay down with
him on the bed

now he lives in a caravan in Sidcup and she lives with a potter
in a kibbutz

Me

I am a soft white porous sediment. I am a form of limestone. I was born under deep marine conditions from a gradual accumulation of minute plates of calcite shed from tiny organisms. I'm made up of the bones of microscopic animals. The weather does not bother me and I do not slump like clay from rain. I can form tall steep cliffs where ridges meet the sea. I can hold lots of water in my body. I can be used to draw on boards as I spill myself over the surface. You can rub me in your hands to stop yourself from slipping. You can use me to mark up the cloth before you cut your suits. You can put me in the paste you use to clean your teeth. Apart from that, there isn't much you'd want from me.

You

You are made from milk. From cows and sheep and goats and buffalos. You can be pressed into different shapes and flavoured with herbs and spices or smoked over oak to make you age less or encased in rind. You are full of goodness. You can be sweet or sour. Sometimes you stink but the stench makes my mouth water. You are rich in culture. But I have to add a bit of bacteria to get you started. You can be full of holes or veined with blue lines. You can be hard with a tang which stains the tongue or fragile, salty and moist, as I crumble you between my fingers. You are best when left to rest in a cool room. But I like you the most melted over something steaming with heat.

Cam And Shaft

When you first met
he was slugging Jameson's
and you were drinking orange squash.
You had a butterfly broach
attached to your jacket,
he had a knuckle duster
tucked in his pocket.
You had a freckle on your cheek,
he had a tattoo of a snake
coiled round his neck.
You loved Cliff Richard.
His bag was Gene Vincent.
You liked gladioli.
He collected motorbikes.

Now you sit in this cafe
having breakfast together
sharing the same pot of tea,
he gives you his mushrooms
you give him your toast.
After all these years
you've been wearing away
like two moving parts
rubbing together
until they stick.

Hook And Clasp

She spends the evenings on the phone,
he sits in the corner of The Rose and Crown.
She eats banana butties for breakfast,
he has black coffee and a JPS.
She can only sleep with the windows closed,
he can only sleep with them wide open.

The last time they went on a date
the number one song was *Hard Day's Night*.
He wanted to watch *The Pink Panther*,
she fancied *The Strangler*.
To this day they've never seen either.
But something has kept them together:
love, company, custom. The weather.

The Meaning Of Love

She was waiting for a client to ring back
she tapped into Google: *What is love?*
the answers she got were:
'What is love' is a 1993 dance track by Haddaway
which was used in the trailer for the film *Monkey Trouble*.
It is also a song by eighties synthpop sensation Howard Jones.
After his contract with Warner expired,
Jones went on to run Nowhere – a vegetarian restaurant.

The phone rang, it was her client.
He was sorry for the delay
but he'd parked the car at Waitrose
to pick up some Parmesan
for tonight's pasta for one.
Ever since his wife had left him
he'd been doing a lot of cooking,
would she like to come over?
'Yes,' she said, 'why not. What time?'
'Be there about seven,' he said,
'and don't forget your apron.'
'I'm not fussy,' he said,
'but I don't like tuna, asparagus or artichoke hearts.'

The Meaning Of Life

Bored one day at work
he typed: *What is the meaning of life?*
into a Google search bar
and got the following results:
The Meaning of Life is an Irish television programme
presented by Gay Byrne.
It is also the fourth studio album
by the German thrash metal band Tankard
and the second track from the fourth album
by American punk band Offspring
and a 35mm animated short film by Don Hertzfeldt.

As he was reading, there was a knock at the door.
When he opened it he saw a pelican smoking a cigar.
'Listen pal,' the pelican said,
'stop all this fucking about and get on with what you're
supposed to be doing.'
So he went back to the dying man in the hospital room
whose life he was supposed to be saving.

Your Lips

When I wake
you've dressed
and left
for work.

Next to my clogged razor

your lips
on a tissue.

Your Bath

You have left
your bath
in the tub,

lukewarm mud
with a film of skin
on top.

I submerge my flesh
into the swamp
of your wash

and watch
the water lift
your tide mark off.

Wanted: A Husband

From a classified ad on the Chinese social network 'Renren'; literal translation.

Never married.
Master's degree or more.
Not from Wuhan.
No rural ID card.
No only children.
No smokers.
No alcoholics.
No gamblers.
No Virgos.
No Capricorns.
Taller than 172cm.
Sporty.
Parents who are still together.
Salary over 50,000 yuan.
Between 26 and 32 years of age.
Willing to guarantee eating four
dinners at home per week.
At least two ex-girlfriends,
but no more than four.

The Earth Is Moving Closer To Its Sun

There are these white birds
that follow elephants around
and they eat, from their dung, the seeds
the elephants haven't digested.
The feathers of these birds are covered in oil,
a sheen that ensures they go untouched
by any of the elephant's filth.

One day I was out walking
when I came across a pile of elephant dung.
As I passed, out flew one of these birds.
A flash of glimmering light.
You are one of these birds — my love.

Your Favourite Tube Station Is Burnt Oak

Your favourite tube station is Burnt Oak. You once went to Alfacar to find the place where Lorca had been shot then took a photograph of a chipped rock and claimed that was the place, putting the photo on Facebook. You are afraid of Robert Murray Helpmann. You have never read *War and Peace*. You think The Reynolds Girls were better than ABBA, but you have no idea what 'I would rather jack' actually means. You don't know your own phone number. You think gardening is fun. You think men should never wear short trousers. *Bagombo Snuff Box* is your favourite book. You think the Church of Euthanasia is a pretty cool idea. You have a T-shirt with 'save the planet – kill yourself' written on it. You want to open a bar called 'The Domain of the King' after the name of the bar in *Mostly Harmless*. You have a dog called Colin. You say fook instead of fuck. You went to a mixed comprehensive school in Chippenham. You like to point out when people say that rabbits are nocturnal that they are in fact crepuscular. You suffer from a very mild form of xerotic eczema which you call winter itch. You think sea snails are beautiful.

The Longest Married Couple

Ralph and Phyllis Tarrant have been married for 77 years, although they actually met 85 years ago. Phyllis was 16 when she met Ralph, a 22-year-old steel worker. Ralph is now 107 and Phyllis 101. They have been married longer than any other couple in Britain. They met on street corners for three years without so much as a fumble. Then it was supper with her parents and a tot of whiskey before bed. They travelled around Scotland in an Austin van, a lilo behind the seats, with a stove and a saucepan to make tea and bacon and eggs. The Tarrants got married in 1933. At 107, Ralph still stays up until the early hours chatting and drinking. Ralph puts his longevity down to a lot of cheese and onion sandwiches and a glass of whiskey every evening. The tabloids tried to treat the story as one of enduring love. They were interviewed recently on television. Ralph was talking about his adventures, clearly animated. The interviewer turned to Phyllis and said, 'he does talk a lot doesn't he.' To which Phyllis said, 'he does. It gets on your nerves.' When asked what the secret was of a such a long marriage Ralph looked puzzled but then said, 'she goes her way and I go mine.'

When I Remember You

I think of that Christmas Eve,
too much brandy and brie
fumbling with your bra clasp.
When I think of you
I think about my eagle earring
lost in the nest of your hair.

I remember a rainy day in a glasshouse.
Don't throw stones, you said,
then took a fist of gravel
and pelted the panes.

When I remember you I smell that perfume
which you insisted was citrus
but reminded me of vodka shots.
And I think about what you said
when I sped for the last train back.

I'll see you next Sunday, I whispered.
I'll hold my breath, you said.

Still?

Are you still walking round in your underwear
and sleeping in the afternoon?
Do you still send out Christmas cards
and forget to say who from?
Are you still looking for that lighter
to torch those dikey cigarillos?

Me. I've stopped writing lists of why I hate you.
I've stopped wanking off to that photograph
with you in just your underwear and a balaclava.
I've stopped cutting your initials into my skin
with a surgical blade.

But, I've kept that lighter full of fuel
and stashed it in my trouser pocket
the one you had engraved with both our names
so that I still think of you
every time I set fire to something.